NICK WARBURTON

# WAR RECORD

*Illustrated by*
Kay Dixey

**OXFORD**
UNIVERSITY PRESS

## OXFORD
UNIVERSITY PRESS

Great Clarendon Street, Oxford OX2 6DP

Oxford University Press is a department of the University of Oxford.
It furthers the University's objective of excellence in research, scholarship,
and education by publishing worldwide in

Oxford New York

Athens Auckland Bangkok Bogotá Buenos Aires Calcutta
Cape Town Chennai Dar es Salaam Delhi Florence Hong Kong Istanbul
Karachi Kuala Lumpur Madrid Melbourne Mexico City Mumbai
Nairobi Paris São Paulo Shanghai Singapore Taipei Tokyo Toronto Warsaw

and associated companies in Berlin Ibadan

Oxford is a trade mark of Oxford University Press
in the UK and in certain other countries

Text © Nick Warburton 2001
The moral rights of the author have been asserted
Database right Oxford University Press (maker)
First published 2001

All rights reserved
No part of this publication may be reproduced,
stored in a retrieval system, or transmitted, in any form or by any means,
without the prior permission in writing of Oxford University Press,
or as expressly permitted by law, or under terms agreed with the appropriate
reprographics rights organisation. Enquiries concerning reproduction
outside the scope of the above should be sent to the Rights Department,
Oxford University Press, at the address above

You must not circulate this book in any other binding or cover
and you must impose this same condition on any acquiror

British Library Cataloguing in Publication Data
Data available

ISBN 0 19 915969 6

Printed in the UK by Ebenezer Baylis & Son Ltd

*Available in packs*

Year 6 / Primary 7 Class Pack (six of each book)   ISBN 0 19 915971 8
Year 6 / Primary 7 Class Pack (six of each book)   ISBN 0 19 915972 6

# Contents

## War Record

1 The Giant Cotton Tree  5
2 The Soldiers Have Come  15
3 Fight!  23
4 Taking it Back  34

## Graffiti

1 Rolf the Pig  47
2 The Wall  52
3 Messages  63
4 A Shadow on the Wall  68
5 A Divided City  72
6 In Memory  79
7 Three of Us  89
8 Over the Wall  93

About the author  102

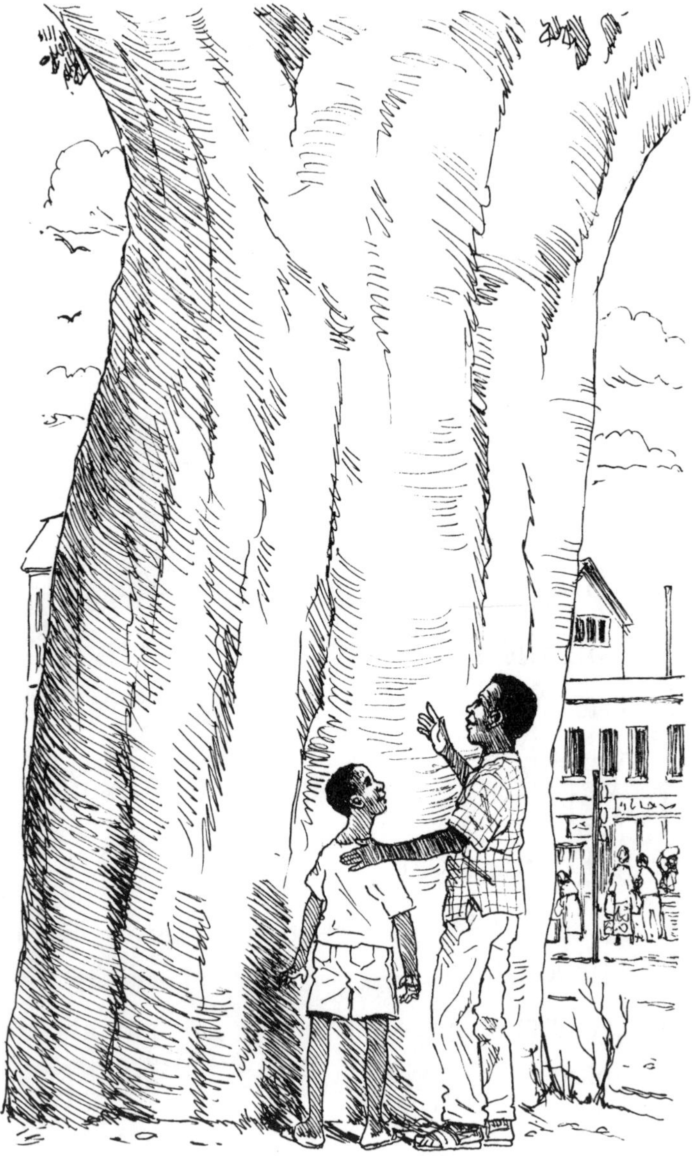

# 1
## *The Giant Cotton Tree*

Momoh sat in the shade of the giant cotton tree at the very heart of town. He rubbed his knee, trying to squeeze the pain out of it. It only helped a little, though, so he leaned back against the tree to rest a while. He sat watching the drivers jolted around in their cars as they bumped over the pot-holes.

The cotton tree was almost as thick as a house and the road passed round it on both sides. A famous tree, it was. Even in his village, miles up country, people knew about the giant cotton tree.

The first time he saw it he was with his

father. They had walked into town to borrow a book from the British Council library.

"Stop and look," his father said. "It is part of our history. Part of the story of Africa."

Momoh didn't understand that. How could a tree – even such a big tree – be part of their history?

"Many years ago," his father explained, "they brought people here to sell them. They sold them as slaves. They roped them together and stood them under this tree and sold them as slaves. Then they put them on boats and sent them away."

"Where did they send them?" Momoh had asked.

"America, the West Indies. That's what they did in those bad old days. They sold people. *People.*"

"But they don't do that now?"

"No. They freed the slaves and sent some of them back. They came back here and started a new country. Our ancestors, Momoh. They made a country of free people, just as it should be."

Momoh wished his father was there to tell him that story again. He remembered the proud look on his face, and his hand on Momoh's shoulder.

"A country of free people, Momoh. Remember that."

But it's not, Momoh thought. People order you about in this country and make you do things. They treat you like they treated those ancestors – like a slave.

He sighed and stood up. No use remembering old stories now. No use sitting under a tree and thinking. He had something to do. He didn't want to do it, but it had to be done.

He looked at the cardboard box resting on his lap. It was old and scuffed and one edge had split open. It wasn't heavy – not at all heavy – but it was still a burden to Momoh. He knew he could not rest until he got rid of it. So, dragging his leg as he went, he crossed the road to the market.

Momoh kept the box tucked against his side because it wasn't his and he didn't want anyone to see it. He shuffled past stalls of bananas and nuts spread out on grass mats, trays of dried fish and rice in thick sacks. On the other side of the market he came to a tall house with wooden shutters bleached pale blue by the sun.

A fine house, he thought. A fine thing to have shutters like that, and steps up to the door.

At the bottom of the steps three boys were playing football with a plastic bottle, and their laughter made him stop for a moment. They were about his age, but Momoh found their laughter strange, like the sound of birds flying overhead, going somewhere else. The boys stopped playing and looked at him, but he shook his head and pointed to the bandage on his leg. He smiled ruefully. No, he couldn't join in with a draggy leg like this. But he didn't want to, anyway. He didn't play games any more – he'd lost the habit.

The boys smiled back and carried on playing. They were using a corrugated iron sheet as a goal, and one of them had propped a book against it. From time to time this boy turned away from the game and went over to touch it with his bare toe.

Well, of course, thought Momoh. It's a library book. Precious. You have to make sure such things are kept safe.

He walked on, up a steep, dusty slope, until he came to the British Council building.

It was large and white and square–another most impressive structure–and it overlooked the town.

A flight of broad steps led up to a glass door. Just once he'd been there before, on the day his father had shown him the cotton tree. They'd stood together on those steps and looked down over the little houses and the market, spread out below like a stitched blanket. And the sea beyond.

The floor on the other side of the glass door was cool against Momoh's feet. It made him panic briefly and forget where the library was, but a man in a clean white shirt showed him the way. In the library he saw a woman sitting behind a tall counter. He went up to the counter and waited. He looked at himself in a brass bell by the woman's elbow, and saw his jaw shaking a little.

"I have come to say sorry," he said when, eventually, she turned to him.

He placed his box in front of her.

"It is a record. To play on a record machine."

The woman picked up the box and slid the record out.

"Macbeth," she said.

"Yes, Macbeth. It is not music. It is people speaking."

"Thank you," said the woman with a quick smile. "But why do you have to say sorry?"

Momoh looked down at the shiny floor.

"Because I should have brought it back a long time ago. It is late."

"I see. Well, you should bring things back on time, you know. People might want to borrow them."

Leaning back in her chair, she pulled a small box of cards from a shelf and flicked through them while Momoh waited.

"Ah, yes," she said. "I thought so. Someone has been waiting for this record. He called last week and the week before."

She took off her glasses and moved the card closer to her nose.

"In fact, this poor man has called five times to ask about this record."

"I'm very sorry. Tell the man I'm sorry to make him wait."

"How long have you had it?" the woman asked, picking up the box and turning it over.

She found the label in the corner and studied it in silence. Then she looked up at Momoh.

"Over a year?" she said.

"Yes."

"You've kept this record for more than a year?"

"I'm very sorry," said Momoh miserably. "Is there a fine to pay?"

"A very big fine for a year, young man. Why didn't you bring it back before?"

"My father borrowed it. He walked from our village to borrow it because our neighbour had a machine to play records on."

Momoh remembered the neighbour with the record machine. His name was James and when he brought the machine back from town he called everyone to come and see it. Most of the village gathered outside his hut and watched in silence as he opened the lid and wound the handle. They stood in silence, watching the plate spin round. It was very impressive.

"And did your father play the record?" the woman said.

"No. The machine got broken."

"Then he should have brought the record straight back. Why keep it in your village if you can't hear it?"

"He was going to bring it back, but he couldn't."

"Why not? If you're spinning me a story, young man..."

"Yes," said Momoh quickly. "I am spinning you a story. But it is a true story."

"Wait a minute, wait a minute," the woman told him.

She stood up and lifted a flap in the counter.

"Come through to the office. A year to bring a record back? You'll need to sit down to explain that."

Momoh followed her into a little room. There were shelves of books all around them. They were walled-in by books. She pointed to a chair at a table and Momoh sat down.

"Now," she said, standing over him and folding her arms. "Begin."

So Momoh told her his story.

# 2
# *The Soldiers Have Come*

More than a year ago it was, the day his father walked into town to borrow the record. Momoh could see himself playing with his friends, some way outside the village. He seemed so small all that time ago. A little boy with his little friends.

He remembered the game they were playing – trying to catch feathers before they floated to the ground – and he remembered laughing. Then there was a sound which made them all stop. It was the crackle of gunfire, coming from the village. They listened and the sound came again. A feather whispered to earth at Momoh's feet and the children looked at each other.

"Soldiers," said Momoh softly. "The soldiers have come to our village."

He said it as if the children had been waiting for them.

Then they ran. They were frightened but they ran back to the village because there was nowhere else to run. Momoh thought about his father, walking back from the town. He prayed that the soldiers hadn't found him.

"Let him stay away," he said to himself as he ran. "Let him be safe."

But if his father stayed away, what would happen to Momoh? He tried to change his prayer but he couldn't think what else to pray for.

They came across people running the other way. The sky was smudged with smoke behind them. He saw James charging towards them, his eyes wide with fear. He was carrying the record machine, struggling with it. When he saw his daughter among the children, he dropped it and it thumped and bounced into a bush. The lid flew open and Momoh saw the plate spin slowly round and stop.

James swung the little girl her off her feet and carried on running. Running away from the village. Then other children were snatched up, or pulled along by their arms, until Momoh was on his own, pushing against the press of villagers.

He shouted at them, "Where's my father? Is he back?" – but no one answered him.

He came to the thorn-bush fence where the goats were kept, and there he saw the first of the soldiers. They were rebels: Momoh knew they would be rebels. He'd heard such bad things about them. The soldier wore a brown jacket, open to the waist, and he had a rifle slung over his shoulder. He was kicking at the rickety gate to get at the goats.

Behind him Momoh saw other soldiers, running this way and that, yelling and firing into the air. Their yells combined with the panicky bleating of the goats as they jumped hopelessly around the enclosure on their frail legs. When the gate caved in the goats sprang at the gap and clambered over each other to get out. The soldier grabbed one by the neck and wrestled it to the ground.

Momoh darted away to his left, so the soldier wouldn't see him. He ran zigzagging further into the village and crouched in the shadow between two huts. A dull rumbling sound came from one of them and the wall was hot to Momoh's touch. He looked up and saw heavy smoke billowing through the roof. Blotting out the sky.

Keeping low to the ground, Momoh crawled along until he reached his own hut. There was a sacking curtain at the door. He yanked it aside and threw himself in.

For a moment the darkness blinded him.

He waited, hoping fiercely to hear his father's voice, but the only sounds came from outside–shouting and screams, bursts of shooting and the roar of fire–and they were all wrong. They made the village strange to him.

When his eyes were used to the gloom, he saw a beaker, tipped over and spilling dark water on the dirt floor. A jumble of blankets. His father's chair, upended.

And a cardboard box.

* * *

"The record," said the woman.

She was now sitting, her hands spread on the table between them.

"Yes," Momoh said. "Macbeth. The record my father borrowed from your library."

"So he was back from town?"

"Yes. He was back, but I still could not find him."

A sudden, clear ringing sound cut through

the air and made Momoh jump. It was the bell on the library desk. Someone wanted help. The sound was like a goad sticking into him and it made him feel bad – he was making this person wait. Probably making him angry.

The librarian gave a short sigh and got up from the table. She walked quickly into the library and he heard her snap at the person waiting by the desk.

"Please," he heard her say. "I'll be with you in a minute."

There was a growling reply. Deep. A man's voice. Momoh couldn't make out the words but he sounded impatient. Momoh looked at the office door. It stood half-open so that he could just see part of the librarian's back.

He thought about getting out. He'd said enough. He'd brought the record back – that was enough. He'd told her about the smoke and the gun-fire; he didn't want to tell her what came next because it was so much worse. So he thought he'd make a dash for the door.

But the woman was returning. She came

back into the little office and sat down opposite Momoh.

"He can wait a while," she said. "Go on."

\* \* \*

Momoh told her how, without thinking, he snatched up the cardboard box and ran outside. And saw his father, struggling between two of the soldiers.

He called out to him – "Father! It's me! I'm here!" – and his father, twisting his head round so the muscles stood out on his neck, saw him.

He shouted back. "Just run, Momoh! Out into the bush. Go!"

So Momoh did what his father told him. There was nothing he could do to help, so he ran. Dust was on his face, and tears in the dust. His bare feet thudded on the ground. A rifle cracked and something whined in the air above his head. He didn't turn to look. He just ran on until the sounds of the burning huts and the gun-shots became faint. They fell far behind him. Then Momoh dropped to the ground. He found he was still clutching the record in its box. The cardboard was splashed with tears.

They didn't come after him. He was only one small boy. They left him to get away. And his father, struggling with the soldiers ...

That was the last he saw of his father.

# 3
# *Fight!*

For days – he could not remember how many days – Momoh wandered around the empty scrub-land on his own. He burned in the sun by day, and shivered with cold at night. He had nothing but his old blue tee-shirt and shorts, and the cardboard box.

He watched the horizon, afraid of what he might see there. When he found trees, he climbed them for safety and tried to sleep, wedged against the thickest branches. But sleep was not easy: he was kept awake by images of the burning village and his father struggling between those men.

One day, he was sitting with his back against a tree trunk, cradling the box in his arms. He was very tired and weak with hunger. His eyes kept closing, closing and closing, until he dozed off. It seemed like only seconds later when he felt a shadow cross his face. He woke up and blinked. Someone was standing over him. A dark shape against the blue-white sky. The sun blazed behind the shape.

It moved a little, briefly obscuring the sun, and Momoh found himself squinting at the green and black patches of a camouflage jacket. It was a soldier looking down at him, and beyond the soldier were others, standing around, leaning on rifles.

At first he felt dull and weary, nothing else. They had found him at last. Well, what did that matter any more? He didn't care.

The man started to shout questions at him and drag him to his feet. Where had he come from? What was he doing? Momoh tried to answer but the words were thick in his mouth and they only made the man more angry.

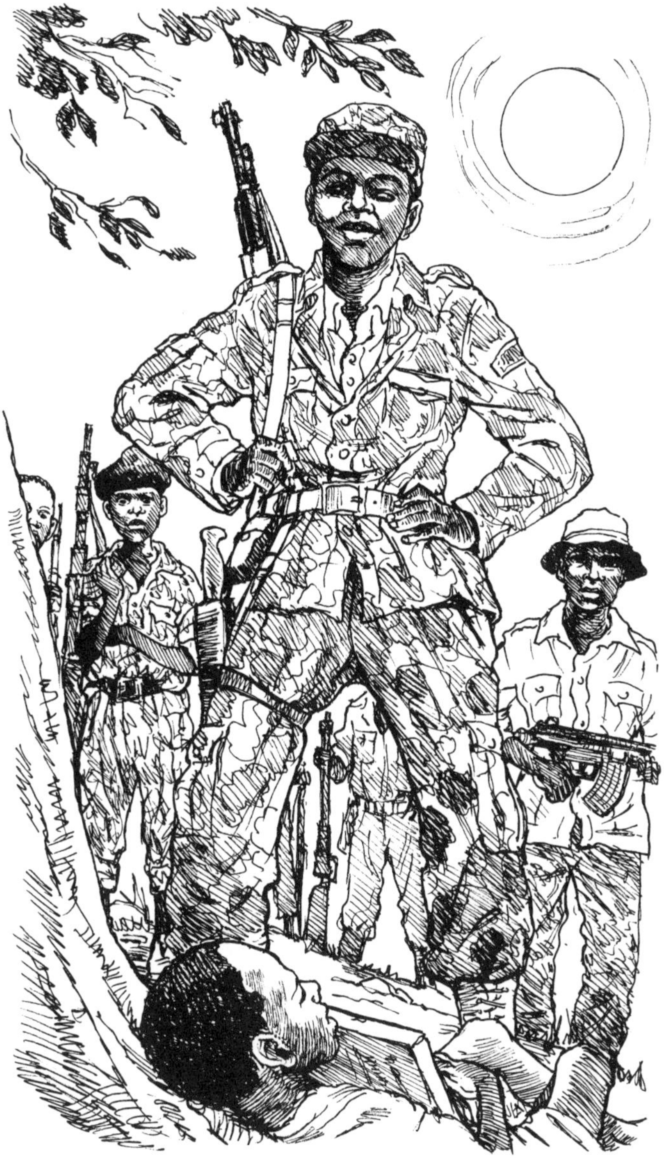

"You come along with us," he shouted, pushing Momoh towards the others.

There were twenty or so in the gang – the leader, Alagba, and six, perhaps seven men. The rest were boys. Most were about Momoh's age, but one or two were even younger. They were all carrying rifles and long knives, just like the men.

Soldiers – boy soldiers.

They were sitting in the dust and waiting. Their faces were the faces of children, but their eyes were blank and lifeless. There was no talk and certainly no laughter. They merely waited.

And Momoh was forced to join them, to become a kind of slave. At first, he was relieved that they had allowed him to live – he was even grateful to Alagba for finding him – but in time he came to think differently. In time he came to wish that he could fall into an endless, empty sleep and forget everything he'd ever seen.

To begin with, though, he was made to tramp through the dry scrub-land with the other boys. No one told him where they were going.

At dusk they stopped to build a fire and eat. Someone gave Momoh a tin plate with a mash of nuts and chicken on it. He was about to eat when Alagba grabbed the plate away. From his belt he took a bullet, and cut it open with his knife. He tipped the grains of gunpowder into the mash and stirred it all together.

"This will make you brave and fearless – a good fighter," Alagba told him.

Momoh ate it – he was hungry enough to eat anything – and when he finished his belly felt good and heavy but his heart was unchanged. He felt no braver, and just as lost and hopeless.

They stayed there that night and in the morning set off across the bare land again – marching, marching – and still Momoh didn't know where they were going or why. Then, just before midday, they saw a clump of trees in the distance and two men watching over a few cattle. The men were waving their arms, as if they were arguing or laughing together.

Then one of them pointed and they both stood still, peering at the little cloud of dust thrown up by the soldiers. As soon as the soldiers changed course, veering from their straight line and heading in their direction, the men began to move. They moved quickly, abandoning the cattle and making for the trees. Momoh heard their tiny cries as they ran. They were shouting warnings.

Alagba ordered the soldiers into a trot.

The trees came closer and soon Momoh could see the grey walls of huts between the trunks. Then people and chickens running in all directions. He knew what would happen next.

They burst through the trees and his ears rang with the sound of gunfire and curses and people screaming for help. The soldiers spread out – they knew what to do – but Momoh stopped running and simply looked about him, rigid with fear. His arms and legs were shaking and he could hear himself sobbing.

Alagba appeared at his side waving a broad knife in his face. He smacked the flat of the blade hard against Momoh's shoulder.

"We are not here to watch!" Alagba screamed. "Fight!"

\* \* \*

He saw men die that day. People who were just like his father and his neighbours. He saw them lying, awkward and limp on the ground, or still alive, covering their heads with their hands and crying. Some he saw running out across the scrub-land, dragging children, leaving everything behind.

When it was all over, he saw charred circles where the huts had been; broken clods of mud; the blackened fingers of burnt trees; blood in the dirt, and flies. That was how they must have left his own village – reduced to ashes and silence. The same noise and panic to begin with, and then smoke settling, almost peaceful.

This time, though, he was not one of those running away: he was part of the cause.

While the others busied themselves finding food and making shelters, Momoh crawled to the edge of the little wood to be sick. He tried to keep himself out of sight. Alagba would be angry if he saw him – a soldier made sick by fighting. He lay there for some moments, hugging his knees and clenching his teeth to stop them rattling in his head, and he found himself looking at the cardboard box.

It was propped against a bush, as if someone had put it there for safe-keeping. He couldn't remember, but he must have dropped it when the firing started.

He stared at it, amazed. It seemed so strange to see it there – a thing belonging to his past, to the time before the killing.

He reached out and touched it with the tips of his fingers. Then he closed his eyes and pictured himself standing by the cotton tree with his father.

\* \* \*

Weeks merged into months and at some point, Momoh thought, a year must have passed. All that time he kept the cardboard box with him. He always knew where it was, even when they were raiding one of the villages.

The men didn't bother with the box – it was no good to them – but once one of the boys tried to steal it while Momoh slept. He felt his fingers being eased open and woke up immediately. Then he became wild, flailing out with his fists and feet. The boy scampered away like a rat and Momoh went after him.

Alagba heard the row and came running over, but when he saw that it was only about Momoh's old box, he looked on and laughed.

"That's good," he said. "It makes him fight."

Momoh got the box back, scuffed a little

but safe. None of the boys ever tried to take it from him again.

\* \* \*

One day, they came to a village larger than usual. Momoh thought it was in the north somewhere but he wasn't sure and, anyway, it didn't matter. It didn't matter where it was. He was with some of the boys, tossing burning branches into the empty huts, when a man fired at them from the shade of a thorn bush.

Momoh felt a sharp slap in his leg.

He crumpled over and, when he tried to get up, he could not make his leg move. The pain throbbed up to his hip and then spread into his whole body till it lodged in his head – a fiery pain that made his head swim.

He looked up and saw flecks of black darting through flames. The sky was turning grey and the flames were scratching against it.

Inside his head was the crackle and roar of burning.

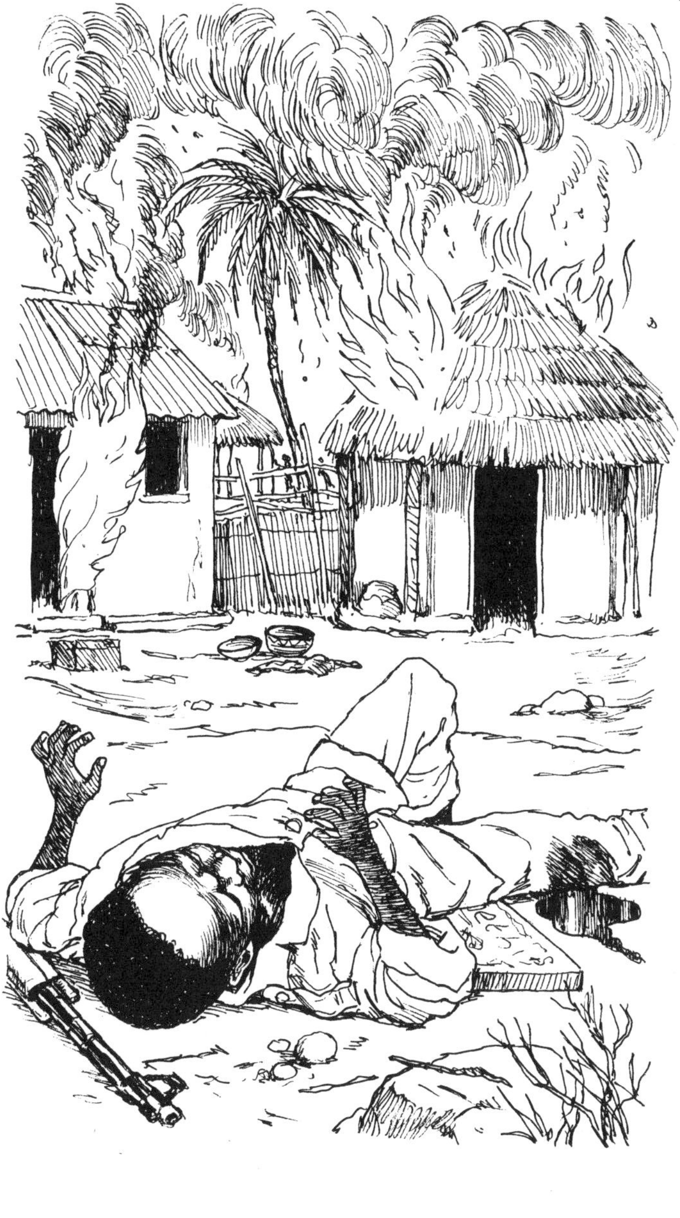

# 4
# *Taking it Back*

He woke up in a long room with white walls. There were two rows of beds in the room but they were empty. He could hear a beating sound, soft and steady, and when he opened his eyes he saw three blades turning on the ceiling. Stirring the air.

Momoh was on one of the cots. And he was wearing different clothes. Clean shorts, a new tee-shirt. A man was sitting there looking at him. A thin-faced man with glasses.

The box, Momoh thought suddenly. Where is my box?

He looked round in a panic but it was

there, quite safe on a chair by the cot. He grabbed it and held it to his chest.

"Can you hear me?" the man said.

Momoh could hear but he didn't answer.

"You're in a kind of hospital. You've been very sick. Do you remember what happened?"

He tried to remember but things came to him in fragments which didn't fit together properly. In one fragment he was being jolted about in the back of a lorry. He could see a square of light, with sky and trees and plains of waving grass in it, all rushing backwards as the lorry bumped along. Then he saw the flames at the hut again, and felt the moment when the bullet hit his leg. The pain was still there but it was dull now, and his leg was bandaged. Who had done that? He remembered soldiers – not his soldiers – lifting him into the lorry.

All these things came back to him but they were in the wrong order. The flames should have come before the lorry, shouldn't they?

"My name is Mr Mwangi," the man was saying. "We found you when the rebels were captured. You've been here for two weeks. Did you know that?"

He paused and Momoh looked back at him blankly.

"Can you tell me your name?"

He still said nothing. Nothing at all.

He went to sleep again and woke up later to find that some of the boys he remembered were now in the long white room with him. It was dark but he could see them huddled in the beds. There were other boys, too. Boys he'd never seen before. Alagba and the soldiers had all gone. He never saw them again.

Every so often, Mr Mwangi, the man with

the glasses, came to sit beside him and talk. Sometimes Momoh listened, and sometimes his mind wandered and he let him drone on. He never answered his questions, though. He wouldn't even tell him his name.

After a few days, Mr Mwangi helped him to get up and walk a few paces, up and down between the beds. And the next day he took him outside, into a yard with boys playing in it. There was a fence round the yard, and a road beyond the fence. Cars and trucks moving up and down the road. Lots of people passing by and talking in loud voices. Tall buildings with glass windows and wooden shutters.

I know this place, Momoh thought. This is the town, where the cotton tree grows.

Somewhere nearby was the library where his father had come to borrow the record. A large white building on the top of a hill. The British Council. He knew it.

\* \* \*

Whenever he slept, he had bad dreams. He

kept seeing his father running up a hill with the cardboard box under his arm. He was looking over his shoulder and shouting at Momoh, "Run! Help me, Momoh! I have to take it back!" – but Momoh didn't run. He stayed where he was, watching his father running hard up the hill but getting nowhere because his legs moved so slowly.

And instead of helping, Momoh lifted his rifle and aimed it at his father's back.

The sound of the gun and his own crying used to wake him from this dream. He tried to stay awake afterwards but it wasn't possible. He slipped back into sleep and the dream started again.

One night he woke up and Mr Mwangi was there, holding his broad hand to Momoh's head.

"What is it?" he said. "What's the matter? Can't you tell me?"

And this time Momoh spoke. He tried to tell Mr Mwangi about the dream.

\* \* \*

"So I have come to bring the record back," Momoh told the librarian. "I had to bring it back because that is what my father would want me to do."

"Of course."

"It is hard to do, though. It reminds me of him, you see. But I was wrong to keep it so long. I kept something that wasn't mine."

The woman reached across the table and put her hands on his.

"Don't worry," she said. "It doesn't matter about the record."

"But it does matter. Someone has been waiting all this time for it, and he will be angry and beat me... "

"No, he won't. I won't let him. I'll explain."

"And what about the fine?" Momoh asked. "A big, big fine, you said."

The woman smiled, but before she could answer, they heard a knock on the office door. It was the man who had been ringing the bell. He was tired of waiting and he was coming to see where the librarian had got to.

"Stay here, Momoh," she said. "I won't be a moment."

She stood up and went out to see what this someone wanted, closing the door behind her. For a little while they talked outside in low voices.

Momoh held his breath and waited. He began to feel sick and frightened. The walls of books were closing him in and he longed to be outside, running down the hill away from this place. He just wanted to leave the library behind, and the record and all his memories with it.

Then he heard the woman call his name.

He turned round. She was standing in the

office doorway. There was a man behind her, looking over her shoulder.

"He is here again," the woman said to Momoh. "The man who keeps coming to see if someone has returned the record. He's come back again."

Momoh got to his feet. All that time waiting. The man would be angry...

"Perhaps you should give it to him yourself," the woman said. She stood aside. Then Momoh stared at the man, confused and still too afraid to speak. But the man wasn't angry. Momoh could see that he wasn't angry.

For several seconds he looked at him in silence.

Why isn't he angry? he thought.

Then he thought, I know him. I have seen him before.

But he didn't dare to believe it until, at last, the man spoke.

"Momoh," he said in a whisper. "Momoh, my son."

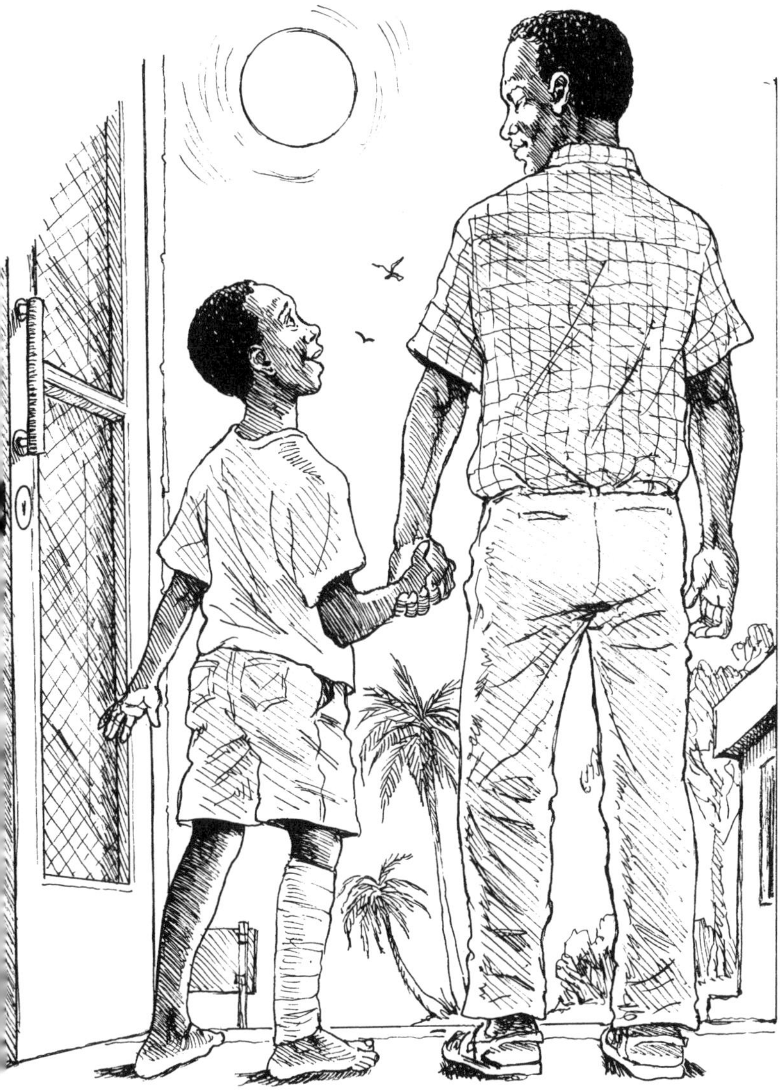

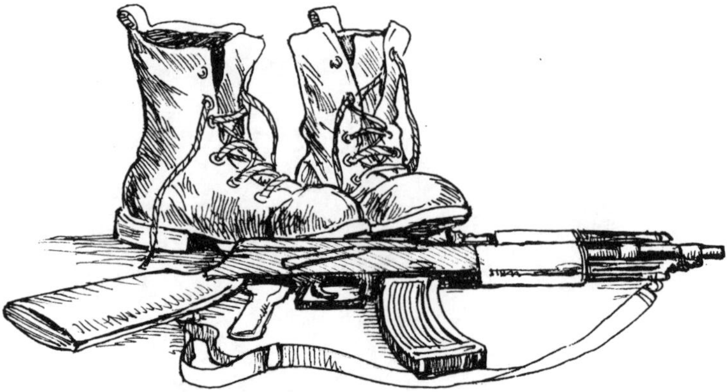

# Graffiti

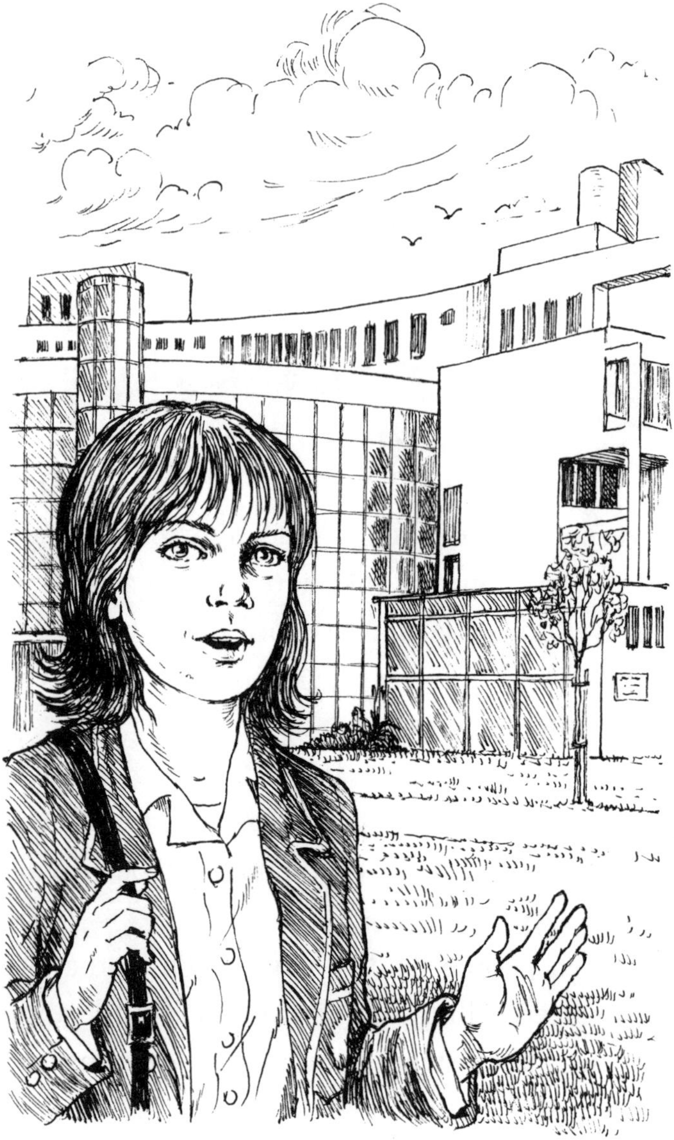

# 1
# *Rolf the Pig*

Everyone's been telling me how lucky I am that Dad's got a job in the city and how marvellous my new school will be. They started telling me weeks ago, before we even moved to the city.

"Oh yes," they said. "That school gets good results, Katrin. You'll do well there. And the city, Katrin – how wonderful to be moving to the city."

Even people who've never been to the city have been telling me how good it's all going to be. They were practically queuing up to tell me.

"So much better than the old school, Katrin. A country school's no good if you want to get on."

As if we did nothing at the old school. As if we all had straw in our mouths and stared at sheep all day.

Well, maybe they're right, but we've been in the city for three days now and I don't like the look of it. And tomorrow I see the school.

So we shall see.

\* \* \*

Well, I've seen it now and I'm not impressed. This school is huge and full of strange people. Not just unknown-strange, but peculiar-strange as well. They look at you as if you're a not very interesting specimen of insect life. You feel like an insect, too, under all that glass. Half the walls are made of hard glass and the corridors all look the same as each other. It's so easy to get lost. In fact, I think they want you to get lost.

I got lost trying to find the dining hall. In the end I heard it: a cheerful rumble of talking at the end of one of those boring corridors. There were two boys lounging by the swing doors. They watched me walk towards them and I knew I was in for trouble.

A couple of big townie louts they were. The sleeves of their jackets were so short you could see their bony wrists. They had plump, shiny faces, both of them. They were well-fed, too, and they watched me all the way down the corridor, all the time smiling in a way that I knew wasn't friendly.

"Ticket," said one of them when I got to the door.

"What ticket?" I asked.

He looked like a snooty pig, if you can imagine a pig with fair hair and dark eyebrows. "You can't come in without a ticket. Don't you know that?"

Grinning at me, daring me to argue.

You don't need tickets to get in to dinner, I know that, but I didn't argue. I'm not stupid. I just went outside to the yard with some of the other sandwich eaters. Except that I didn't have any sandwiches. So that was lunch – huddling against a wall and trying not to look cold and hungry.

I found out the head lout's name. It's Rolf.

I didn't tell Mum about missing lunch. She wants me to like my new school and I don't want to disappoint her. She wants me to like the city, too. So much more to do here, she says. Better than the country in every way. More people, more friends.

"What friends?" I want to ask, but I don't.

She can see what I'm thinking, though.

"Give it time," she says. "You'll get used to it. The city can offer all sorts of things, Katrin."

At the moment it offers me dirt and noise and unfriendly people. They're sharp and out for what they can get. They eye you suspiciously, as if they're working out what they can get out of you.

Anyway, it isn't even true that we live in a city. We live in half a city. There's a wall running right through the middle of it. From top to bottom. East one side and West the other, and the Wall between. West is good because that's where we live. East is a terrible place. The people who live there are grey and dull and they live in grey, dull buildings. They have no freedom. So everyone says, anyway.

"No freedom," they say. "Imagine."

What I imagine is that they say the same things on the other side of the Wall. They probably think the West is a terrible place.

How does anyone know what it's like on the other side? And what sort of freedom do we really have here? What's so wonderful about the West when they don't even let you eat your lunch?

# 2
# *The Wall*

I saw the Wall for the first time today.

I was on my way out of school at the end of a boring day, when I saw Rolf the Pig and his grinning friend loitering at the gates. No point asking for trouble, I thought, so I turned round and went out the back way. The long way round.

I found myself in a street that took me further and further away from where I wanted to be. I kept taking left turns, hoping they would lead me back to somewhere I recognized, but they didn't. So I took a few right turns. Above the rooftops I could see a church spire and I used that to keep track of where I was heading.

I came to a corner, went round it and there was a broad stretch of scrubby grass. I could see a few spindly trees and some dried-up bushes. More bushes formed a low hedge along the boundary of the churchyard. There was a tall, silent church away to my right, with a make-shift banner hanging limply over the doors: *We're a thousand years old – come and celebrate with us!*

Across the open space, beyond the church, was the Wall.

I stood there for ages, staring at it, amazed. It was so unexpected. A row of tidy, ordinary houses, then the scrubby ground and the church, and then the Wall. A towering construction of rough breeze-blocks and bricks. An ugly thing, not properly designed but botched together. There were square look-out posts every few metres. Tangled wire ran along the top which was wide enough to walk on. I couldn't see this from where I stood, but I noticed guards moving silently from post to post behind the wire. They say people sometimes try to cross the Wall. East to West, and West to East. I thought that was a bit odd at first – crossing the Wall both ways – but maybe they do it because it's there, like some mountain waiting to be climbed.

A wall. An ugly great wall.

This is more like it, though. It's the only thing about the city that they don't like, but it interests me.

\* \* \*

Rolf and his friend weren't loitering at the gates today, but I went the long way home anyway. I wanted to see the Wall again. I'd been thinking about it all day and I wanted to see if I'd remembered it properly.

I hadn't. There were a few things I hadn't noticed before. For one thing, I'd remembered it as straight – a massive thing cutting right through the city in a direct line. It wasn't. The bit I saw followed a wide curve round the church, like a solid river of stone.

Then there was the graffiti. It's strange that

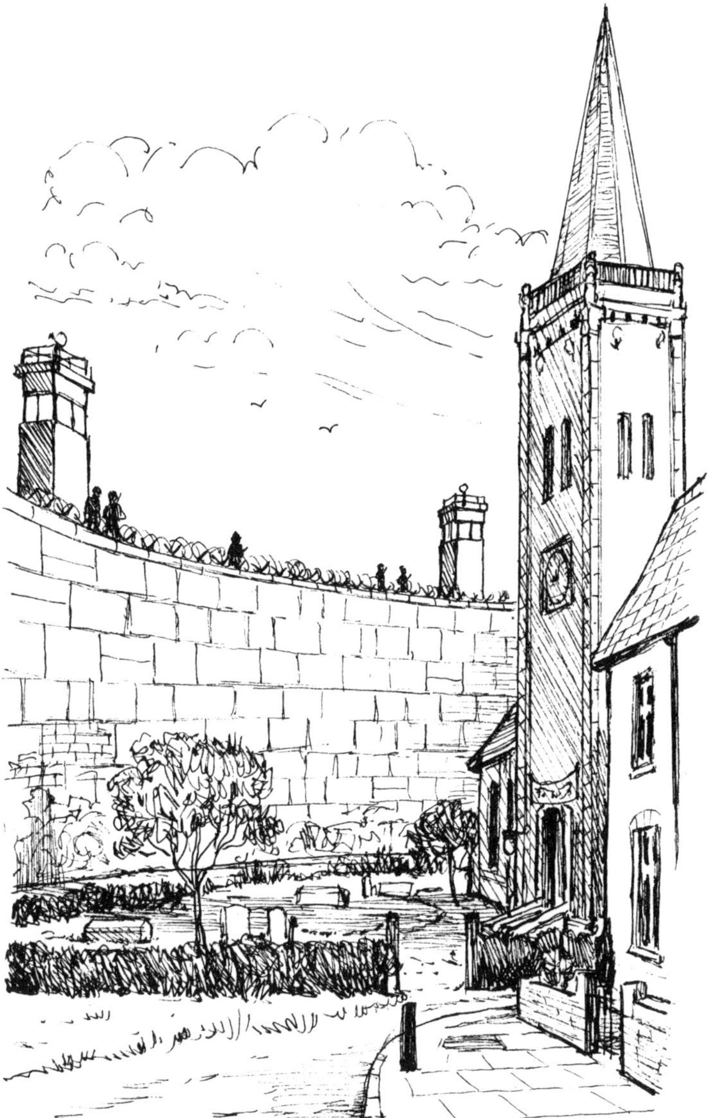

I didn't notice the graffiti yesterday – it seems so obvious now – but I suppose I was just awe-struck by the size of the Wall, by the surprise of it. In several places it had letters and pictures painted on its rough surface. Decorated words and patterns jumbled together and overlapped in a mass of colour against the grey. There were single words in thick blocks of colour outlined in black. Some were names and some just words; strange words, some of them. I didn't understand what they were supposed to mean. Someone had written "FREE AIR" in a fluffy white cloud. There were pictures, too. Mostly animals – snakes and dogs and dragons – which curled and twisted round a small door.

I thought that was odd – an ordinary house door in that great thickness of wall – until I realized that the door was painted, too. It was very skilfully done. It had a small round window with curtains and a single word painted on the letter box: "EXIT".

I stood for quite a while, staring at all this from the other side of the open ground. Then

I crossed to take a closer look. There was no one about, but I'd only gone a few steps when I heard someone shouting:

"Stop there! Don't come any closer!"

It was one of the guards. He was peering down at me from the top of the Wall. The click of the safety catch on his rifle rang out across the space between us. I stopped walking and held my hands up.

"Only looking," I called up to him.

"Don't. There's nothing to see. Now get back."

So I went back. I studied the wall for another five minutes or so, and then I started for home. And all the time I was wondering: how can people write on the Wall if they're not allowed near it?

\* \* \*

After supper, I said I was going out for a walk. Mum looked surprised and asked where.

"I'm going to meet Heidi," I said.

Then she looked pleased. Heidi? So she's making friends already.

Heidi doesn't exist, of course. I was going back to the Wall. There's something about the place which draws me to it. Maybe because it's so different from our street. Everything there is normal and respectable – the pastor of the church lives a couple of houses along from us – but the Wall is kind of wild.

I found it quite easily this time, using the church spire to guide me. It's certainly not beautiful, apart from some of the graffiti, but it fascinates me. This city is like a hundred others: same shops and traffic and burger bars. It's grimy and loud and all set out in order. Same people going about the same sort of things. Except it has the Wall. And the Wall makes it different.

It was dark when I got there. Autumn dark, thickened by fog and mist. I thought I might be able to get closer and study some of the graffiti, but that was impossible. There were searchlights probing the mist from the look-out posts. Solid beams cut through the fog. First one way and then the other, in long slow sweeps. Most of the time they lit up the open ground and the bushes, but at the point where the Wall curved they were able to play along its length for about twenty metres.

This time I wasn't alone. A couple of people were sitting on the steps by the church doors. They were lit by a cone of orange glow from a lamp above the doors and it looked as if they were eating sandwiches. Just sitting there, as if they weren't even aware of this great wall behind the church.

It was only when the lights hit the Wall that I could see the graffiti, and then only for a few seconds. Otherwise all I could make out was the bulk of the Wall, winding away into the dark, a monster crouching down to sleep. In the distance I could hear the whine of traffic.

Then, as I was about to come away, I saw two shadows break away from some of the church trees in a darting run. It was the sandwich eaters. One searchlight beamed away to the left, reached its furthest point and began to move back. Another was sweeping back from the right. Between them was a gap of darkness, and the two figures moved in this.

When they got to the Wall they flattened themselves against it in a kind of safe spot. I guessed they were boys but I couldn't be sure. They were dressed in dark clothes. One had a scarf wrapped around his head and the other wore a jacket with a hood. I moved back behind one of the trees and watched them through the gloom.

They took out cans and began to spray the Wall. They worked quickly and kept looking up to check on the progress of the searchlights. When the lights came close they stopped work and hid in the bushes for a moment. Then carried on. I couldn't see what they were painting, though.

It was strange to see them, so busy and intent. And strange, too, that they chose that particular bit of the Wall to paint – the only part that could be seen clearly from the lookout towers.

* * *

I set off early this morning so I could go the long way again and see what the boys had painted. I was expecting some fascinating new pattern so I was disappointed when I saw it. A few letters and some numbers in a decorated border. They didn't make much sense to me.

RGK – 18-10-88

I guessed the numbers represented a date – last week, in fact, – so the letters might've been someone's initials. Probably one of the boys who painted them. Or maybe both of them – their initials combined. It seemed an odd thing to do, though, to go to all that trouble, and take all that risk, just to paint initials and dates. If I was doing it I'd paint something people would really notice. Another animal to go round the door, perhaps.

That's when the idea hit me. I could paint something on the Wall myself. A pig, I thought. For everyone to see. With a label round its neck – Rolf the Pig.

Then I remembered the guard shouting down at me, and the dangerous click of his rifle. It would be a foolish thing to do, really. Foolish and risky.

But it would be exciting, too.

# 3
# *Messages*

I've persuaded Mum to let me take sandwiches for lunch. The two louts are on duty every day and they stop anyone who looks a bit timid and go through the ticket routine. I think they get money out of some of them. I just keep out of the way. I don't want to waste my time with stupid arguments there's no chance of winning. Besides, I have better things to think about.

I've been out to meet Heidi every evening this week. Which means, of course, that I've been working on Rolf the Pig! It's incredible. All day I'm thinking about the time when I can get back to the Wall.

I started by blocking in the body. I couldn't get any pink paint so my pig is light brown. It's not very good paint, either. A few downpours of rain and poor Rolf will be washed away. That won't matter, though. I'll just start something else. I've painted him as if he's jumping over the door. A flying pig, with his ears pinned back.

When I went back to him after my first night's work, I found that someone had written a message on him. I didn't notice at first because the writing was so small. It was neatly written on Rolf's back leg and I'm sure they meant it just for me because you can only read it when you're almost on top of it. I guess it was written by the sandwich eaters. I've seen them a couple of times, sitting under the lamp-light on the church steps before they start work.

'Nice pig,' the message says, 'but don't paint here. This is our pitch. Move along the Wall.'

I'm not moving, though. Whoever they are, it's not their Wall. It belongs to everyone.

* * *

Rolf is getting to be the most magnificent pig you've ever seen. I'm really proud of him. Before I started work on him tonight, I wrote a little message on one of the patterns the two mystery painters have been doing. I thanked them for their message but I said I intended to carry on with the pig. It was a friendly message, but it let them know I won't be ordered about. I get enough ordering about at school: I don't see why I should put up with it here.

Then I got on with the real art work.

I was concentrating so hard on getting Rolf's dark eyebrows just right that I was almost caught by the lights. I dived for the bushes and lay there with my chest heaving, afraid that I was stirring the leaves and that I'd be noticed. But they didn't notice me.

They'll never see me. I'm leading a charmed life. I feel sure of it.

It's like a game. What's the time, Mr Wolf?

Rolf is nearly finished now. I've put a label round his neck. All I have to do is add the name. And then think what to do next.

\* \* \*

I didn't have time to do any painting tonight, but I went to the Wall to take a look at my handiwork.

Some more peculiar symbols and words had appeared. I can't see the point of that. If you're going to paint things people can't understand, what's the point of painting at all?

There was also an answer to my message.

We're not ordering you, we're asking you. And this is not a game. What do you think the door is for?

It felt strange reading that, almost as if I could hear their voices. A conversation with people I don't know. Like having pen friends. They seem friendly enough but I don't know what they mean about the door. It's a door, just as Rolf is a pig. What else could it mean?

Anyway, if they're not going to explain what they mean, how can they expect me to give up?

# 4
# *A Shadow on the Wall*

Then everything was different. The painters were right: it's not a game.

The Wall changed for me and I swore I didn't ever want to go again. The pig wasn't finished – the label was still empty – but I wasn't going back. This is how it happened.

When I got there the next evening, the other two were already at work. The same two who wrote me that message. As far as I could tell, no one else painted on the stretch of the Wall by the church. It was a clearer, warmer night so I didn't mind waiting, but they were taking ages. I began to wonder whether I should cross over to the Wall and join them, or go home and come back the next evening. In the end I decided I couldn't wait. I'd run over and start work on the label.

I don't have to speak to them, I thought.

But before I could take a step, there was a disturbance further down the Wall. Shouting and the sound of boots on stone. Running along the top of the Wall and the rattle of rifles.

I saw the beams of light jerk and swing towards the sounds. They picked out a spot about fifty metres away to the left. A rope was dangling from the Wall, as if it had been thrown over from the other side.

A man was clinging to it. Desperately thrashing

his arms and legs. A huge spider of shadow danced on the Wall beyond him.

There was a shot and the man dropped with a tiny cry. I saw him writhe on the ground. He writhed and then he stopped. Very still. One elbow sticking up at an awkward angle.

Perfectly still.

It became very quiet. I heard the guards talking to each other. Their voices were calm and normal. All in a night's work.

I was fixed there, staring, unable to move, when the two painters came running across the corner of the churchyard towards me. They were stooping low. As they ran past, one of them hissed at me.

"Run," he said. "Get out of here!"

\* \* \*

I tried to put the Wall out of my head but I couldn't stop thinking about the man they shot. I kept seeing him, lying in a pool of light, his elbow twisted as if he was trying to shade his eyes. Eyes that would never see again. I keep seeing his shadow dancing on the Wall.

I began to understand what some of the graffiti meant.

```
RGK - 18-10-88
```

I guessed they were the initials of someone else who died trying to cross the Wall. And the date of his death. It was a kind of memorial.

I had never stopped to think what happened to people who failed to cross the Wall. Or why they even tried it. I thought they did it as some kind of dare. It was more than just a dare, though. They had to be desperate.

```
RGK - 18-10-88
```

It meant someone. A person. It puzzled me that they knew his initials, but they must've found out somehow, I suppose.

I realized then what the door means, too. It wasn't just a picture – it stood for something. Escape. A sign of hope.

# 5
# A Divided City

The other day Dad came in looking very pleased with himself. He had a large cardboard box tucked under his arm. He put it on the kitchen table and solemnly took the lid off while Mum and I watched. It was full of fireworks.

"Look at these," he said. "I was lucky to get them: they're in great demand round here, you know."

"Why?" I said.

"Because of the celebrations at the church. It's a thousand years old in a couple of weeks," he told me. "Everyone's been buying fireworks. Lots of people are taking things along to help the celebrations. Food and things, too. We're taking these."

"We don't go to church, though."

"Well, I was thinking we should. It's a way of joining in with the community, isn't it?"

He was proud of his fireworks and he brought the pastor in to have a look at them. I thought that was embarrassing, showing a grown man fireworks, but the pastor was impressed. He stood in our kitchen, gazing down at them with his hat in his hand, like a man looking at some fantastic picture in an art gallery. He shook Dad's hand when he left and said it would be nice to see us in church on Sunday.

"You will," Dad said in his jolly voice.

"Why not?"

It was the last thing I wanted to do, though, because it would take me back to the Wall. But I couldn't tell Dad that, so on Sunday we all got dressed up and went to church. As we walked up to the big double doors, I kept my eyes on the gravel path and tried not to look at the Wall. It was impossible. It loomed there in the corner of my eye till we got inside the church. After the service, we waited to chat to the pastor and shake his hand.

"Glad you could make it," he said.

"Lovely church," said Dad. "And so big. You can see the spire for miles."

"Perhaps you'd like a quick trip up the tower? You get the most fantastic views of the city."

We struggled up a spiral staircase, the pastor first, then Dad, then me, with Mum puffing behind, all of us clinging on to the stone wall as we went. On and on we climbed until at last we stooped through a little door and emerged into the air and the light. We were on a narrow walkway which ran round the base of the spire. I looked up at the spire and it seemed to be moving against the grey-white sky. It seemed to be slowly toppling.

"My word," said Dad. "Come and look at this."

He was on the other side of the walkway, grasping an iron railing with both hands and gazing out over the side. I shuffled round to join him and saw the city stretched out below us like a faded carpet woven with intricate patterns. The Wall cut right across it and I could see the other side for the first time. A few boxy cars moving slowly along broad roads. Tiny dots of people. It didn't seem very different from our own side of the Wall. Houses like ours, avenues of bare trees. Perhaps it was slightly shabbier over there, as if the carpet had been folded in half so that one side had become more faded and worn.

I saw the bend in the Wall below us, and the graffiti which I'd helped to paint. That stretch of the Wall, I noticed, could be seen from some of the houses on the other side.

They'll be able to see what we put, I thought.

Then I saw military lorries and armoured cars trundling up and down by the Wall.

"There, you see," said the pastor in a quiet voice. "A city divided by a wall – people kept apart by guns."

And once again the image of that poor man came back to me. I tried to imagine what he must've felt when he tried to climb the Wall –the hopelessness of it all. I wondered about his family. Did he have parents? Children? Was that why he'd risked so much? So that he could join them?

"I expect you know," the pastor went on, "that many poor souls try to cross that dreadful Wall. Sometimes we even hear the sound of gunshots during services."

"Do any of them make it?" I asked.

"A few, Katrin. Most don't. It's a desperate thing to try. You can be shot if you even approach the Wall. Sometimes we've been able to give a few of them a decent burial, though we don't know their names if they

77

come from the other side, of course."

I wanted to ask if he'd given a decent burial to the man I saw, but I couldn't let them know where I'd been. All I could do was hope that someone had taken proper care of him. It would have been a sad affair, though, even so. Only strangers to mourn for him.

Coming away from the church I changed my mind about visiting the Wall again. I decided I would go back. Not to paint silly pigs, but to make him a memorial.

# 6
# *In Memory*

At school today I took my sandwiches into the dining hall, as I'm entitled to. Rolf and the other lout were there as usual and they stopped me and launched into the same stupid ticket routine.

"I don't need a ticket," I told them.

Rolf smirked and said I'd have to pay if I wanted to eat. So I looked him directly in the eye and told him to grow up. Then I pushed past and went in. I wasn't scared and I think he could see that I wasn't. He shouted something after me but he didn't follow. He let me go. I shan't bother to avoid them again.

I shall go where I want to go and they won't stop me.

\* \* \*

It was very different, being back at the Wall that night. Now that I knew what it really meant, I was a lot more frightened. I looked over my shoulder all the time, checking on the lights. But I had to do it; I had to go there. There had to be a memorial.

I began by scrubbing out the pig. I planned to replace it with a simple box, like the one the others painted except that I would decorate the edges of mine with leaves of laurel. I'd found some small tins of glossy paint in Dad's shed. The colours were limited – only blue, white and green – but the paint would last. No rain would wash it away.

In the box I planned to write *In memory of an unknown man* and then put the date. I set to work, using a strip of cardboard to get straight edges. It was important that the box was as perfect as I could make it. All the lines had to be straight and of an even thickness.

That's what I was doing when they came for me. I kept checking on the movement of the lights, but I didn't think to listen. So I didn't know they were there until one of them spoke.

"What happened to the pig?"

My heart leapt at the sound of a voice so suddenly close and I smudged the paint as I turned round. I recognized them at once – one with a scarf round his head and the other with his hood tied tight round his face. They were kneeling behind me, about a metre away. I stared at them and said nothing.

"What happened to the pig?" repeated the one with the scarf.

He did all the talking. The other didn't say a word unless he had to.

"I washed it off," I said. "Why?"

"We've been watching it grow. Did you see our messages?"

"Of course. Anyway, the pig's gone now. That's what you wanted, wasn't it?"

"No. It's not that. What are you doing now?"

"Same as you," I said. "A memorial."

They looked at each other briefly. Then the silent one caught sight of something and nodded towards the searchlight. It was moving slowly back towards us. We scuttled over to the bushes and stayed there till it passed.

"How do you know what we're doing?" the one with the scarf asked when we were in darkness again.

"I guessed. And, look, you've made me smudge my line. I can't get rid of it, you know. I'll have to change the design."

"No. Leave it."

"Leave it? Why should I?"

He didn't answer but reached out his hand and took me by the wrist.

"Come with us," he said.

"No. I can't. I have to get home..."

But they ignored me and began to hurry back to the cover of the church, crouching as they ran and pulling me with them. I had to follow. It would've been stupid to struggle out in the open ground with the guards patrolling the top of the Wall.

We reached the safety of the church and they stood for a moment, looking at me so intently that I became worried. I'd always thought they were wall-painters, like me and dozens of other people I never saw, but how could I be sure? The Wall seemed so dangerous now. Maybe they worked for the other side. Maybe they'd been sent over to check on the people who ruined their Wall with graffiti.

By the orange glow of the lamp over the church doors I could at last make out their faces. Thin, pale faces framed by hood and scarf. Shadow obscuring their eyes. They were older than me but not by much. Old enough to be at college, I guessed. They told me their names. Karl was the one with the scarf; his friend's name was Michael. There was something about the way that Michael looked at me, with a kind of simmering anger, that frightened me.

"What do you want?" I asked them. "I haven't done anything wrong."

"Painting's wrong," said Karl. "They don't like it."

"It does no harm. I only—"

I stopped myself. I was going to tell them about the memorial for the unknown man, but suddenly it didn't seem like a good idea. It seemed best to tell them nothing.

"You only what?" he asked.

"Nothing."

"We left you a message asking you to move somewhere else. This is one of the most dangerous parts of the Wall. Why do you come here?"

"I didn't know it was dangerous when I started."

"But you know now."

"Yes."

"And you still come back?"

"Yes. I've got used to it. I like it. Anyway, what's it got to do with you? The Wall isn't yours, is it?"

He smiled.

"If it was mine I'd tear it down," he said.

Again he looked at his friend. It was a questioning look – can we trust her? After a moment Michael's hood moved in a slow, deliberate nod.

"Right," Karl went on. "You say you know what we're doing, but I don't think you do. This is more than painting pictures and writing words... "

"They're memorials," I said, "for those who try to escape."

"Yes, they are. Sometimes. But not only that. Who else knows you're here?"

My mind raced before I answered. If I told them the truth – that no one knew I visited the Wall – I would be putting myself at their mercy. Even if Mum and Dad worried and came looking for me they wouldn't think of coming to the Wall. But I thought there was something in Karl's face that I could trust.

"I always come alone," I said. "I haven't told anyone I come here."

"All right, then. Listen carefully. I'm going to explain why we want you to move. But you mustn't tell a soul about this. Not a soul."

I nodded.

"We work on this part of the Wall because it's one of the few places where people on the other side can see what we do. They see what we paint and know that they have friends on this side. They can also read messages."

"Messages?" I asked. "What sort of messages?"

"What do you think?" said Michael shortly.

It was the only time he said anything without being asked a question first.

"They're messages about escape," said Karl. "Anyone who climbs the Wall without planning it first hasn't got much chance of getting through. They do it sometimes, of course, because they're desperate, but they hardly ever succeed. If we can tell them exactly where and when to make their attempt, though, they have some hope. We can arrange to meet them. We can distract the guards. That's why we paint – to send messages. And when you come along and add your bits, you confuse things. You think you're not doing any harm, but you are."

He paused and glanced at Michael before going on.

"Michael's brother lives on the other side,"

he said. "We're planning to get him out."

I shook my head, unable to speak. My foolish squiggles and daubings might've ruined their plans. Someone might've died because of them. I felt sick to my stomach at the thought. Karl smiled and squeezed my arm.

"Don't feel bad," he said. "You weren't to know."

"What can I do?" I said, turning to him. "Tell me how I can help."

# 7
# *Three of Us*

Of course, Karl and Michael said there was nothing I could do to help.

"Just keep out of the way and don't tell anyone," Karl told me. "We know what we're doing but it's going to be dangerous."

"You'd be in the way," Michael said.

I wanted to help, though. I owed it to them for all the trouble I'd caused. And I had an idea how we might get Michael's brother safely to this side. If I could persuade them to listen to me, I was sure they'd let me help them.

I went back to the Wall that night and

watched and waited from the shadow of the church. I didn't go to paint. I wasn't going to do any more of that until all this was over. Then I would finish my memorial. It would be the last thing I did there.

They didn't turn up. So I went back again the next night, and the next, and the next, until I saw them.

\* \* \*

They were there this time. I just caught sight of them scurrying away from the Wall as I arrived.

They went to their usual place, under the lamp-light by the church door, and sat down with their backs against the stone steps. They sat there in silence, staring up at the night and breathing in cold air. I went over to join them.

"We've just finished the last piece of the jigsaw," Karl told me. "Everything's ready now."

"When?" I asked. "When will it happen?"

Michael drew his knees up to his chest and rested his chin on them.

"We'd be crazy to answer that question," he said without looking at me.

"And you'd be crazy not to listen to me," I said. "I think I can help."

Then I told them about my idea. And they did listen, although, for a long time, they made no response. Michael continued to hug his knees and look straight ahead of him at nothing.

"What do you think?" I asked.

"I don't know," said Karl. "It sounds risky."

"Not as risky as what you'll be doing. And you have to admit, it'll be a lot easier with three of us."

Karl still looked doubtful – I think he was about to say no – but Michael got in first.

"Yes," he said slowly. "It might work, yes."

"You mean, you'll try it?" I asked him. "You'll let me help?"

"Yes," he said, "we'll let you help. But don't go getting yourself shot. That'll be no use to us at all."

# 8
# *Over the Wall*

Mum chose that night of all nights to question me about Heidi.

"Who is she exactly?" she said. "Why haven't we met her yet?"

"Heidi? She's very shy," I said weakly. "She doesn't like to go out."

"Well, I want to talk to her, Katrin. I'm not happy about you going out all the time. And so late back sometimes."

"All we do is chat, though, Mum. We do our homework and talk, and we sometimes lose track of the time."

"Even though I warn you about being late."

"I won't be late tonight, I promise."

"No, you won't, because you're not going out tonight. In fact, I don't think you'll be going out again until we know a bit more about this Heidi."

"But she's expecting me."

"I can't help that, Katrin. You are not to see her again until you bring her to the house so we can meet her properly."

And that was that. There was no point arguing. I know what she's like when she gets like that. I felt bad because I don't like deceiving her. Not about Heidi, I mean. I had to make up Heidi so I could get away to the Wall – that's fair enough. No, I felt bad because I knew that I would go out tonight whatever she said.

I had to. Michael's brother was coming over the Wall that night.

I hoped she'd forgive me. I was sure she'd understand if she knew about Michael's brother. She wouldn't let me out, but she'd understand. I hoped Dad would forgive me, too. I hoped that, when this was all over, he'd be able to see exactly why I had to take his precious fireworks.

\* \* \*

Karl and Michael were beginning to think about alternative plans when I joined them at the church. I explained that it was difficult to get away, that I had to get the box and wait for a chance to sneak out unseen.

"So they're suspicious," said Michael. "And they'll come looking for you."

He was on edge. We all were. I was tingling with fear and excitement at what we were about to do.

"They won't miss me yet," I said, "and

when they do, they won't think of coming here."

"If we're going to do this," Karl said, "we'd better get on with it. We've got seven minutes. You know where to go?"

I nodded but he went over it again anyway.

"Beyond the church about fifty metres," he said and pointed away to my right. "The bushes are thicker there. Stay in the bushes and you shouldn't be seen. Don't take any risks, Katrin. Light one firework and drop it in the box..."

"I know, I know," I said.

" ... then get back to the church. If they all go off we'll make our move. If not, the whole thing's off."

I snatched up the box and moved out of the cover of the church. A cool breeze was blowing directly into my face. I was fairly sure I wouldn't be picked up in the searchlights, but all the time I could feel the seconds ticking away, the moment coming closer. I moved as near to the Wall as I could without breaking free of the bushes. Then I dumped the box

97

down and removed the lid, crouching over it with the matches ready. But when I looked at my watch there were three and a half minutes still to go. And those minutes crawled and dragged. I almost persuaded myself that my watch had stopped.

But slowly the time arrived. Turning my back to the Wall, I struck a match. It flared, suddenly very bright, and went out. I took a quick look at the Wall and saw the guards still pacing steadily along the top, the lights still making their slow sweeps.

My fingers were trembling and I dropped the next match. The third one took. Cupping my hand, I held it against the twist of blue paper at the end of the biggest firework I could find. The match went out but the paper caught in a tiny red glow.

Not enough, I thought. It's going out.

I was supposed to head straight back to the church but I couldn't. I had to wait and see.

Silence and darkness.

Then the first soft fizz of silvery sparks. I saw a tangle of sharp shadows light the inside of the box. Then I turned and ran.

There was a crackle of explosions behind me. The searchlights swung round at once and began to probe the bushes. The guards came clattering and shouting along the top of the Wall. One stopped and fired a rifle in the direction of the fireworks.

We knew it wouldn't take long for them to guess the fireworks were only a trick. Karl and Michael would have to move quickly.

I felt my feet scrunch on the gravel path and knew I'd reached the safety of the church. I stopped running and looked back. A cloud of purple smoke was drifting towards me. Through it I saw a blur of yellow flame where the box had caught fire. But one of the guards was already making his way back along the Wall, shouting angrily over his shoulder.

He was too late. I heard footsteps on the gravel, turned and saw Karl and Michael hurtle round the corner. Between them was a third figure. He fell back against the church wall, lifted his head and gasped for air.

Free air.

No one spoke. We crouched there, the four of us, listening to the fireworks. We held hands and watched the light flashing over the bushes and against the bulk of the Wall. Red and blue and silver scribbled on the darkness like bright new graffiti.

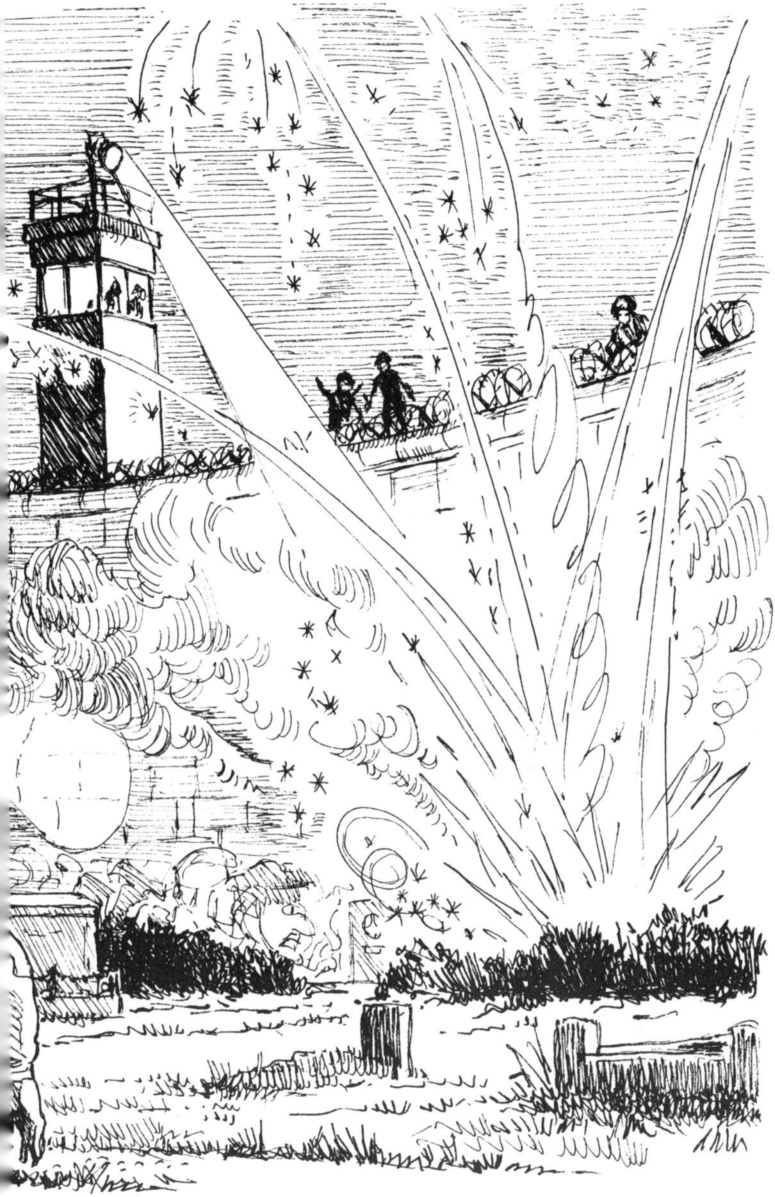

## *About the author*

As well as stories for children, I also write plays for stage, radio and television from my little office in Cambridge. In 1992 I spent a short time working for the British Council with other writers in Sierra Leone, West Africa. The idea for *War Record* came from a story told to me there. As I write, that country of brave and friendly people is being torn apart by civil war and the horrors which Momoh saw and experienced are being repeated.

The second story, *Graffiti*, is also about civil war. Katrin does not live in Berlin, although her city is like it in many ways.

For many years, Berlin was divided by a wall which kept ordinary people apart – parents from children, brother from sister and friend from friend. However, there are many other cities in the world – Belfast, Jerusalem, Johannesburg to name just three – where people have been prevented from living together in harmony. Walls of politics, religion, poverty or race divide them. Katrin's city is like these.

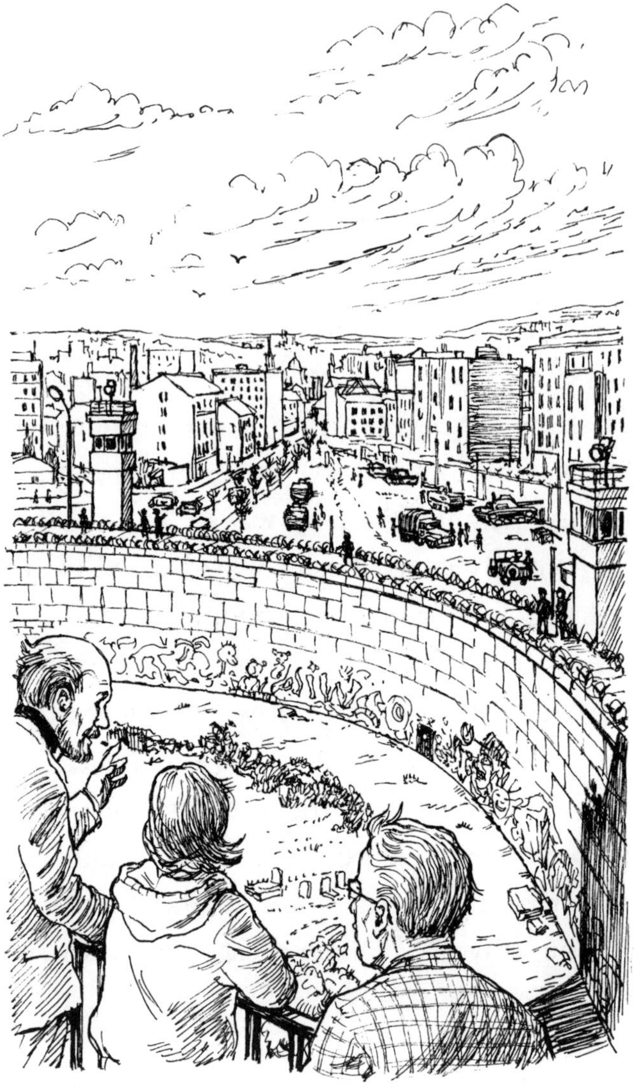